KV-675-837

Writing for kicks

The language of Football

We shall not, we shall not be moved!

We shall not, we shall not be moved!

Just like a team that's gonna win the FA Cup!

We shall not be moved!

'And we all know that in football if you
stand still you go backwards ...'

Peter Reid, Tyne Tees Sports Special

Written and compiled by Jim Sweetman, writer and English consultant
Edited by Adrienne Jones and Jenny Rhys
Illustrated by Nick Pearson

Print ited

For more details about the Writing For kicks television programmes go to: www.4learning.co.uk/secondary

Who this book is for!

This book has been written to accompany a series of television programmes called **Writing For Kicks**, broadcast by Channel 4. The aim of the book is to look more broadly at football, at the extraordinary variety and richness of writing that is linked to the game. The subject matter provokes books, plays, poems and songs; pages of newsprint are devoted to it and it provides a driving force for metaphor. Football is embedded in popular culture but constantly surprises us with its capacity for reinvention.

Young people of all ages, from small children to teenagers, play, watch and read about football and as an activity it offers a point of entry to an adult world. This book is about a social, cultural and leisure activity that young people engage with as part of becoming adult. Because the subject matter can be discussed equally validly in academic theses or workplaces, and because anyone can play it, football is a point where the world of adults and the world of young people can easily and comfortably overlap.

For reluctant readers and writers of all ages the overlap makes football a rich seam for exploration. This is the real world where any piece of writing has a whole range of purposes and audiences.

None of the literary material in this book was 'written for kids' or for use by teachers. It is culled from all sorts of sources, most of which have football in common. The Go for Goal! sections are for people who want to understand a bit more about the power of writing and to try out something different for themselves and the Manager's Tips offer some hints on how to set about being a better writer. Use them if you like or if your teacher suggests it, but otherwise just take a minute to enjoy the some of the fantastic writing associated with the game of football.

Jim Sweetman

LOCATION: LRC

COLLECTION: Loan

CLASS MARK: 428 SWE

BARCODE No: 520979

DATE: 12/05/05

Contents

Playing at Wembley

There is nothing to match the sensation that hits you when you walk from the mouth of that tunnel. The first sight is like a horseshoe made out of tens of thousands of faces amid dazzling colour. All those faces … peering among the flags. I looked around and it was a mass of red and white like a wall from the Royal Box right round to the other. Bloody hell! But then the blue and yellow Wimbledon support brought together like never before, bless their hearts. 'Not bad this.' I thought. 'Not bad at all.'

As the national anthem played we stared straight at the Liverpool players and they looked away uncomfortably. It wasn't pre-planned but a spontaneous thing. They were singing the anthem and looking anywhere but straight into our eyes.

I can't even tell you who kicked off. The first thing that springs to mind was Andy Thorn getting tied up with Peter Beardsley, the referee blowing his whistle but Beardsley carrying on and putting the ball in the net. He probably heard the whistle, anyway, but it was an early scare.

John Barnes had a scoring chance and I knew I had to get there to stop him. I went in shoulder to shoulder, bosh – sheer strength that swept the ball away and barged Barnesy as well. He looked at me as if to say: 'You want it that much do you?'

For 20 minutes we worked our socks off, didn't let them win the midfield, shut them down, didn't let them play the way they wanted. Don Howe's words were going over and over in my mind and then Steve McMahon had the ball. I always had this impression of McMahon in possession – receiving the ball, opening up and switching the play. As he shaped to receive it, I started running at him knowing exactly what I was going to do, picking up pace and saying to myself that I'd never get a better chance. I knew he wanted to stamp his authority on me and rattle me as quickly as he could.

I made up my mind to gamble that he would let the ball come across him and open out with it on the inside of his foot. If he'd just

Write your own player's eye view of the final moments of a big match.

Go For Goal!

That's how Vinnie Jones saw Wembley Stadium and the FA Cup Final in 1988 when Wimbledon played Liverpool as the underdogs and won. It's the player's eye view of a big game and very different from what television shows us.

stopped that ball I would probably have been sent off. If he'd just touched it backwards, I'd have buried him. I gambled on meeting him head-on with a proper solid tackle on a ball. It turned out just like reading a book. As I arrived he opened up, lovely, and my momentum took me in – wallop! I met the ball and saw his legs go up in the air. I was on the ground looking up at him as he was coming down on his back.

Some pro, Steve McMahon. Even on the way down, he was thinking, and as he landed he caught me with his elbow underneath my left eye. It split and bled and the mark still shows sometimes. My lifelong reminder of a close encounter on the sacred turf!

Vinnie: The Autobiography,
Vinnie Jones

MANAGER'S TIP

What makes Vinnie's account compelling reading? Think about how everything is seen through his eyes and how what he notices is different from what a commentator or even a camera would see. What is written down here are the thoughts that go through his mind as the big game starts. Look at how sounds and colours bring the game to life. Do the same in your own writing. Don't try to write about anything more than a few minutes of the game.

Hit the Headlines

This is the football headline generator. It could be used by every newspaper in England – and you can learn about English grammar at the same time!

This headline generator can produce around a million different headlines, most of which make sense. If you use it, you'll be writing a complex sentence containing a prepositional clause!

STEP ONE

Start with an adjective	Your club's name	Throw in a verb
amazing	Arsenal	crash
brave	Bolton	fail
brilliant	Chelsea	lose
crippled	Ipswich	play
disappointing	Leeds	rise
dreadful	Liverpool	survive
gallant	Man. United	struggle
lucky	Newcastle	suffer
magnificent	Spurs	triumph
plucky	Villa	win

STEP TWO

An adverb	Pick a preposition	A phrase
bravely	against	a whisker
deservedly	by	better opposition
heroically	down	bitter contest
meteorically	for	extra-time drama
pointlessly	from	foreign heat
poorly	in	hard-fought battle
superbly	over	local derby
tragically	to	old rivals
unexpectedly	under	skin of their teeth
weakly	with	superior odds

Go For Goal!

If it's the football season, collect together a set of football headlines. See how the headlines from different newspapers compare and look at how they use adjectives, verbs and nouns. Next, develop your own set of headlines for your favourite team.

MANAGER'S TIP

Try a few variations on the headline generator model. You can make a good headline with just a noun and a verb, for example, or you can start the headline with a preposition and phrase.

Liverpool on fire as Sunderland crash and burn

Tate's Great!

Outstanding Orient leap to the top

Dirty Leeds lose the plot

Woeful Everton hit rock bottom

Spurs and Bolton scrap ends in a stalemate

Majestic United cruise to victory

Striker returns to haunt Newcastle

Arsenal's carelessness costs them dear

Ipswich surprise cocky Villa

Stuttering Chelsea scrape a point

FOOTBALL *Poets*

People might think that football and poetry don't go together but they're wrong. In fact, there are plenty of fans who write poems about their clubs, players, good and bad moments, and their feelings about the game.

Below are two very different poems by Crispin Thomas. The first is about a football legend of the 1950s, Stanley Matthews, while the second pokes fun at the footballers of today.

STANLEY MATTHEWS

The Ghost of Stanley Matthews

Late in the game when the fog
swirls in
And you long for a rub of the dice
You pray that some figure will
dance through the mud
And cause havoc out under the
lights

For legends and myths are like
rivers
But there's one that will last for
all time
And I swear that I've seen him
appear through the mist
Drifting like smoke down the line

And some here among you will
nod and agree
And to some it is nowt but a
name
But the ghost of the sweet
Stanley Matthews
Still hovers around this great
game

Yes I swear that the ghost of Sir
Stanley
Still lingers on many a ground
With his bright orange shirt and
his parting

When footballs were heavy
and brown

Yes I've seen him at Wembley, at
Stoke and at Ayr
On muddied old parks coming
out of thin air
Just ghosting past players as if
they're not there
For he had a class so refined – in
his time

And when I look out on a cold
cold day
In a fifties and throwback and
sad kinda way
I can still see that swerve – I can
still see that sway
For Stan was an idol of mine –
and so fine

And maybe his shorts did come
down to his knees
And maybe his hair was all
Brylcreemed in grease
But there ain't a crowd that our
Stan didn't please
But he's left us and gone now –
long gone

And he probably went home with
tuppence a week
For all that he did for the game
But he stood for a time and a
working man's sport
That is sadly no longer the same

But his ghost lingers on in the
good things
Whatever – wherever they are
And I dare you to try to compare
him
For Sir Stan was a true soccer
star

And some here among you will
nod and agree
And to some it is nowt but a
name
But the ghost of the sweet
Stanley Matthews
Still hovers around this great
game

Crispin Thomas

What's So Wrong About Wanting To Marry A Big Soccer Star?

So what's so wrong
about wanting yeah
To marry a big soccer star
And what's so wrong
about shed-loads of
money
And shed-loads of clothes
and a car

Cause you know what you
get when you're sorted
With your nice little
footballer man
You get fat weekly
wages for starters
That bring in at
least twenty grand

And the chance to live
somewhere in Essex
In a typically Mock-Tudor home
With totally footballer furniture
Just a nice massive place of
your own

Yeah cos I need a guy with the
minimum taste
And footballers sure fit the
picture

And maybe they're not
all that clever upstairs
But I tell ya they
don't come much richer

MANAGER'S TIP

See how the first poem uses four line verses and rhymes to carry the reader along and to convey the idea that this is a poem about the past, while the second is more modern and conversational in style and asks questions. It also has a neat ending.

Stuck for ideas? Start with a famous footballer you like or someone not so famous. Tell the story of their great football moment. Or, write a poem asking 'Would you like to be a football player in today's game ...?', or a commentator, or a sports reporter!

Yeah and I need a guy who goes fishing
Or maybe plays golf at the worst
One who dishes out diamonds and oners*
Whenever he open his purse

One who opens up big supermarkets
And leaves me alone on weekends
So I can go clubbing while he is away
With one of his nice popstar friends

Yeah and I'd like to get off with Giggsy
Or that David Beckham he'd do
Maybe drive in a Roller with David Ginola
Or lovely Les Ferdinand too

I'd draw the line if they're married
I don't want no grief in my life
I wanna go far in the Sun or the Star
But not being chased by some wife

And I'd never shack up with Gazza
Or Jason 'Shampoo' McAteer
No I wanna live with a nice soccer star
And I reckon that I'm getting there
But there's only one problem that bugs me
And I feel I'm a bit of a joke
It's like I'm heading this ball up against some brick wall
Because I'm not a girl I'm a bloke

Crispin Thomas

* a 'oner' is £100

Go For Goal!

Use either of these poems as a model for one of your own. It need not be as long but try to catch the same mood in your own verses.

Ian McMillan

Ian McMillan writes poems about football for his local paper. Below is what he said about the referee in one match before he wrote a poem about him:

When you're a football poet, you don't just write about the players, because referees are great subjects for poems because they're kind of in charge, and they're shouting, and they're running up and down.

And this one here – he's really good. He's got a bald head, which is always good for a referee, but also he's got a fantastic expressive face. A bit like a mime artist. I think he enjoys this. I think referees enjoy being in charge. They get a bit of abuse, but they enjoy it. It's a bit like a poet enjoys being in charge of a poem. Good idea that. I think I'll write it down.

Fantastic game this. There's a thing happening down there where all the players are gathering around ... and pointing and shouting and the ref's got his card out. He loves it ... he loves waving it, the king of the card. But he's calling across his linesman now, and the other one – like three black crows on a wire as a poet might say. And they're all pointing and shouting. Oh that's what I like – a bit of argy bargy – good for a poem.

THE REFEREE

And here's his poem.

Referee

Who's that bloke
In the black
With a whistle
Who looks like he's
Been sat
On a thistle?

Who's that man
With the cunning plan
To do all the daft things
He possibly can?

Referee! Referee!
Take advice from folks like me
Referee! Referee!
We can see things that you can't
see!

Who's that bloke
In the black
With a whistle
Who looks like he's
Been sat
On a thistle?

Poets

Who's that feller
Waves red and yeller
We'd be better off
With me Auntie Bella!

At least she knows the rules!

Referee! Referee!
That was never a penalty!
Referee! Referee!
You should have booked that
number three!

He comes on the field
Carrying the ball
Strutting like
He's 10 feet tall.
And for 90 minutes
He's in charge
Handing out the order
Giving it large

He's like a teacher
He's the boss
And you can't say anything
To him because
Out will come
His little black book
A lick of his pencil
And your name's been took!
He's waving yellow
Waving red
I bet he takes his whistle with
him
When he goes to bed!

Who's that bloke
In the black
With a whistle
Who looks like he's
Been sat
On a thistle?
Do you wish I was you
And
You
Were
Me?

Ian McMillan

**His poems can be more
serious too ...**

Try 'Stadium' on the next page.

Stadium

There's no hint here, now,
Of the noise to come
This is … rows of emptiness,
Waiting

This is like a beach before the tide comes in,
This is like a cup before it fills with tea
This is like a face before it starts to grin
This is like a stream before it rolls to the sea …

Here come the people
Into the stands
Here comes the water
Across the sand
Here comes the swelling
Seething crowd
Laughing, shouting,
Excited, loud …

And the game kicks off and the waters rise
And there's a storm going on before your eyes
Waves of attacking, players surfing tackles
As the atmosphere's electric, the stadium crackles.
Some players sink and some players swim
And some could do with rowing in a well appointed gym!
But the game is the sea, and the crowd is the boat
As excitement grips you in the belly and throat!

And there it goes,
Draining away
Like light at the end
Of an autumn day
Drifting back
Like an ebbing tide
From packed inside
To cold outside,

This is like a beach when the water's gone
This is like a cup when the drink's been drained
This is like a face with no make-up on
This is like a stream after months without rain.

There's no hint here, now
Of what's just been,
This is … rows of emptiness,
Waiting.

Ian McMillan

13

Poems about football can also be sad. This is a more difficult poem but it's about more than football. Think about how the son feels.

Falling from grace in the eyes of a child

No longer the brash-booted hero out of myth
stands the father, faced down by
the crowd of youths who won't return
the football. His only son
knows tears are close; self-pity
rising to the throat; witnesses
a cloudy day in Spring
the godhead's irreversible
defeat.

Wandering home beneath a shrinking sky
they dare not speak the knowledge they have shared.

Tony Lewis-Jones

Just Because I am a Ball

Just because I am a ball
Does not mean I lack feelings at all.
I get kicked around
When I'm on the ground,
And I cry when I'm high
Right up there in the sky,
And I despair, there,
Hanging in the air,
And I'm full of woe,
When they kick me through the snow,
I suffer to my cost,
When tackled by Jack Frost,
It goes against the grain,
To play football in the rain,
I get booted in the air
And the lads don't even care.
Just because I am a ball
Does not mean I lack feelings at all.

Chandelle Joynes

Ball

Every match is the same,
The fun, the anger, the pain,
Football boots and turf,
More trouble than it's worth.
As I get kicked up to the sky
I think why oh why
Do I have to suffer the pain in the wind and rain.
I wish I could be a member of the team,
I still remember that one day it will all end
And then I can rest and mend.

Carly Spencer

Old Ball

I wish I wasn't a ball.
I'm sitting on my own,
Feeling all alone,
Then the boys come pick me up,
And I begin to roam.
But it's no fun being a ball,
Being kicked around all day,
I'm getting bruised and battered
From constant use and play.
I'm losing all my pressure,
My colour's going too,
Soon they'll put me in the bin,
And buy a ball brand new.

Louise Gardner

Go For Goal!

These three poems which take a football's view of the game are all by schoolchildren. Could you do as well, or even better? Write your own poem or poems – start by writing your own about a ball, using what Ian McMillan says to help you.

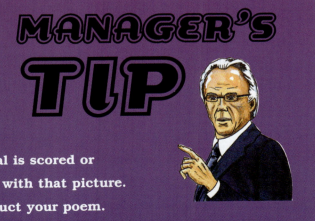

MANAGER'S TIP

When you're writing a poem, don't just sit and think. Instead, use a sheet of paper to jot down your thoughts and ideas in any order as they come to you.

If you're stuck, think of a picture – the crowd pushing through the gate, the moment when a goal is scored or disallowed – then think about the feelings that go with that picture. Get plenty of notes down and then start to construct your poem. Think of it as a picture in words.

My Father's Eyes

There's an old story, and maybe it's true and maybe it isn't, about a skinny little boy who loved football with all his heart. In the street or the park, day in and day out, he gave everything he had, but being half the size of the other boys, he got nowhere.

When he joined the local boys' team, he found himself left on the bench more often than not and he hardly ever played. As a teenager, this boy lived alone with his father but the two of them had a great relationship and even when the son was on the bench, his father was on the line cheering. He never missed a Sunday morning game.

The boy still loved football and, when he moved to a new town to work, he decided to join the local team. It was a small club in a local league but the manager took a shine to the boy because of his enthusiasm and because he always put his heart and soul into every practice. If nothing else, he encouraged the rest of the team with his infectious support.

His big day arrived out of the blue. Injuries and a bout of food poisoning for four of the regulars meant he was in the team for that Saturday afternoon and in a qualifying round of the FA Cup, too. He might have been a grown man but he rushed like a boy to the nearest phone and called his father. He was perplexed and worried when the phone just kept ringing and he was at the ground when the next telephone call came. The manager let him take it in the office. His father had died in the early hours of the Saturday morning. 'Don't worry about the match,' said the manager, as the young man's face crumpled in boyish tears.

Go For Goal!

Write your own football story with a twist at the end like this. Think about what could happen in extra time or a penalty shoot-out. What about 'giant-killing' where a team surprises better opposition? Remember that girls play football too!

Keep your story simple but make sure that it builds up to an exciting climax. Create a character that your readers will like. Use description, conversation and feelings to keep your story interesting.

MANAGER'S TIP

Kick-off arrived and passed, and the Cup tie was not going well for the team. Then, after 75 minutes, when the home team was two goals down, a silent young man slipped quietly into the empty changing-room and put on his kit. As he ran out onto the sidelines, the manager was astounded to see him and even more surprised when the young man begged to be allowed on as substitute. Thinking things could not get any worse for the team, or the player, the manager agreed.

'All right,' he said, 'you can go on. Do your best!' But, within minutes, the manager, the players and everyone watching were rubbing their eyes in disbelief. This little unknown, who had never played in the team before, was doing everything right. The opposing team simply could not stop him. He ran, he passed, he shot and tackled like a star. His team began to see they had a chance. He scored, then there was a free kick just outside the box. Two-all. In the closing seconds of the game, the slight young man intercepted a pass and ran all the way to the opposing goal. The keeper never had a chance and the underdogs were through to the next round.

His team hoisted him onto their shoulders but no one could quite believe what had happened. Finally, after the ground had emptied and the rest of the team had showered and gone to celebrate in the nearby pub, the manager noticed him sitting quietly in the corner all alone. He walked over and said, 'I can't believe it. You were fantastic! Tell me what got into you? How did you do it?' The young man looked at the manager with tears in his eyes and said, 'Well, you knew my dad died, but did you know that my dad was blind?' The young man swallowed hard and forced a smile, 'Dad came to all my games, but today was the first time he could see me play, and I wanted to show him I could do it!'

THE ART OF FOOTBALL
Commentary

COMMENTATING

Football commentating is not easy. You have to know the names of all the players (not just those in the teams you support) – and how to pronounce them, who's not playing, where the teams are in the league or cup, the team's tactics and, most importantly, when to speak and when to stay silent.

> **'I never make predictions and I never will.'**
> *Paul Gascoigne*

WHO'S THE BEST?

Martin Tyler is Sky Television's main commentator and has been covering football matches for over 25 years, including every World Cup since 1974. He previously worked for ITV and has commentated on some memorable games, including England qualifying for the World Cup finals in Rome in 1997.

HERE'S ONE VIEW OF HIS PLACE IN HISTORY

Many people think that Sky's Martin Tyler is our best football commentator. John Motson has good background knowledge and quotes facts in detail but sometimes this appears trivial, while other commentators use the match as a vehicle for their own opinions. By contrast, Martin Tyler deploys fine judgement in his use of facts and statistics. He has as many opinions as anyone else, but he doesn't ram them down our throats.

Because Martin was once a player himself, he knows how hard it is to pass, turn and shoot while tough opponents are bumping, tugging, kicking and obstructing – so he is sympathetic towards the players.

While his regular partner Andy Gray is an enthusiast, Martin seems very laid back. He knows the value of understatement and silence. If you listen carefully, there is a kind of genius in what he doesn't say. Above all, Martin is focused on this match. He is passionately interested in this match. While many commentators allow their minds to wander, and start reminiscing about other topics and other matches, he always, always, always finds interesting themes, angles and details in the match he is talking about.

> **'And there's Ray Clemence looking as cool as ever out in the cold.'**
> *Jimmy Hill*

MANAGER'S TIP

Practice and prepare but don't try too hard. Your commentary needs to sound fresh. Jot down four or five little comments that you want to include and tick them off as you use them when the play slows down.

Go For Goal!

Try audiotaping your own football commentaries onto a videotape of your favourite team playing the last five minutes of a big match. It's much harder than you think!

SCHOOL FOR FOOTBALL Commentators

Lesson 1: Talk about this game!

Lesson 2: Talk about this game!

Lesson 3: Even if it's dull, keep talking about this game.

Lesson 4: Don't apologise if there's no goal in the first 35 minutes.

Lesson 5: Don't call it a chess match. Most of the audience cannot play chess. If they could, they would know that chess can be very exciting.

COULD YOU DO BETTER?

You have to talk for 90 minutes, nothing much is happening on the pitch and there are thousands of people hanging on your every word. And then – you go and say something really silly!

'The Uruguayans are losing no time in making a meal around the referee.'
Mike Ingham

'...and the news from Guadalajara where the temperature is 96 degrees, is that Falcao is warming up.'
Brian Moore

'Celtic manager Davie Hay still has a fresh pair of legs up his sleeve.'
John Greig

MATCH Reporting

Here's a match report, written by a trainee reporter on an important FA Cup game between West Ham and Tottenham. Read it carefully.

**West Ham United   2
Tottenham Hotspur 3
Attendance: 26,048**

That's that then. It's the end of the season for the Hammers – or as good as. Their league position is middle of the road, so everything depended on a good FA Cup run, and on Sunday that Cup run came grinding to a halt. After the away victories against Manchester United and Sunderland, the Hammers had every reason to hope for great things from a home tie. But it was not to be. Spurs held on in a pulsating second half to secure a narrow victory. And they held on with a determination that they have rarely shown all season.

It had all looked so promising before the game. We even had the announcer letting fly with Henry V's pre-battle speech about 'Harry and St George'. But for one Harry at least – Harry Redknapp – the day was not to end in triumph. After the match he was visibly deflated. He knew this was West Ham's big chance to keep the pot boiling, but the result had gone the wrong way, and while Spurs fans went rejoicing back to Tottenham, the Hammers

supporters, and Harry (and, possibly, St George), were stunned into silence.

Spurs made the better start. They were quickly into their stride and it took an imperious tackle by Stuart Pearce to frustrate Ferdinand as he was poised to shoot. What a player! What an example to the West Ham youngsters! No wonder Harry Redknapp will sing the man's praises to the rafters. He may be in the twilight of his career, but he can still muster a passion and a drive that are unmatched. By all accounts, he had no chance of playing two days before the match because of the state of his ankle, but people like Pearce don't obey the normal rules. This was the Cup and he was going to play. Joe Cole, Michael Carrick and Frank Lampard have bright futures in front of them, but if they have any sense, they will learn and profit from Pearce's inspiring example. The man is a model professional.

Spurs continued to press in the first half and after 29 minutes their persistence paid off. A prodigious throw from Freund found Rebrov unmarked and the Ukrainian, who has taken so long to find his touch, struck home a sweet volley. West Ham, to their credit, kept scrapping away. Their midfield trio was not being allowed the space that they had enjoyed at Old Trafford and Sunderland, but the whole team kept plugging away. In the 39th minute they had their reward.

A free kick was awarded just outside the penalty area. Up came the inevitable Pearce and in went the inevitable goal, from a thunderous left-foot drive.

One-all at half-time. Things looked as though they could be about to turn around but it was Spurs once again who started the half better. First it was Ferdinand, rising imperiously above Stimac, to head down for Rebrov to complete the move and then Doherty headed in from a corner. Cole, alas, went walkabout. Redknapp was reluctant to blame him after the match, but Cole was clearly at fault in not clearing the ball. Three-one to Spurs. The tide had turned in favour of Tottenham but, just when you might have expected them to coast home, West Ham got into their stride. By now the rain was sheeting down, and Harry Redknapp brought on Todorov, another attacker, to add to the attacking power. It worked.

In the 72nd minute, Cole's pass ricocheted off Young allowing Todorov to score his first goal in English football. And now the stage was set for a tumultuous final stage. Wave after wave of claret and blue hurled itself at the Spurs goal but the Tottenham defence, with keeper Sullivan outstanding, withstood everything the Hammers could throw at them. It took two tremendous saves from Sullivan to keep them out. First he made an instantaneous reaction save from Todorov and then he dived to his left to keep out Freddie Kanoute's drive with one hand.

A tremendous end to a tumultuous FA Cup tie, but not the end that West Ham had wanted. So near and yet so far. The West Ham bubble had burst.

Go For Goal!

Use these questions to focus on the article:

- **What is its key message?**
- **How does it set the scene?**
- **How many different ways can you find of saying that 'a player kicked the ball'?**
- **How are the two teams described without using their names?**
- **Find places where adjectives are used to make the writing more exciting.**

Now you could write your own report. Watch a match, make notes and then start writing. Set yourself a limit of 400 words. Although it is not usually the reporter's job, add a headline.

WEST HAM UTD:
Hislop, Schemmel (Todorov 68), Winterburn, Dailly, Stimac, S. Pearce, Lampard, Carrick, Cole, Di Canio, Kanoute.
Unused subs: Forrest, Moncur, Song, I.Pearce.

Bookings: none.

TOTTENHAM HOTSPUR:
Sullivan, Perry, Young, Campbell, Freund, Clemence, King, Iversen, Rebrov, Ferdinand (Korsten 88).
Unused subs: Walker, Etherington, Davies, Gardner.

Bookings: Sullivan, Clemence, Doherty, Ferdinand.

WORD GAMES

It's not big and it's not clever, but it's amazing what's hidden inside some of football's biggest names. Try a few of your own!

FIRST DIVISION STRIKERS
Lee Hughes – Huge heels
Andy Hunt – Handy nut
Craig Hignett – Great itching
Shaun Goater – Area shotgun

GROUNDS
Goodison Park – Spooking Road
City Ground – Dingy Court
Carrow Road – Coward Roar
Ashton Gate – Ant Hostage
Filbert Street – Better Trifles

Managers and Leaders

What is good leadership? Just how do team captains and managers encourage their players? Leadership is one of the key themes in Shakespeare's play, Henry V. Henry's role as king has a direct parallel with the captain's or manager's role in football – both Henry and many football managers discover that being a leader can be an isolating experience. But there are other ways, as Shakespeare shows when Henry is about to invade France and needs his troops to rally for the fight:

> 'The ideal ... would be someone who could lead from the front, who was big and strong and powerful but also technically aware to organise his army strategically.'
>
> *John Barnes*

Once more unto the breach, dear friends, once more;
Or close the wall up with our English dead.
In peace there's nothing so becomes a man
As modest stillness and humility:
But when the blast of war blows in our ears,
Then imitate the action of the tiger;
Stiffen the sinews, summon up the blood,
Disguise fair nature with hard-favour'd rage;
Then lend the eye a terrible aspect;
Let pry through the portage of the head
Like the brass cannon; let the brow o'erwhelm it
As fearfully as doth a galled rock
O'erhang and jutty his confounded base,
Swill'd with the wild and wasteful ocean.
Now set the teeth and stretch the nostril wide,
Hold hard the breath and bend up every spirit
To his full height.
On, on, you noblest English.
Whose blood is fet from fathers of war-proof!
Fathers that, like so many Alexanders,
Have in these parts from morn till even fought
And sheathed their swords for lack of argument:
Dishonour not your mothers; now attest
That those whom you call'd fathers did beget you.
Be copy now to men of grosser blood,
And teach them how to war.
And you, good yeoman,
Whose limbs were made in England, show us here
The mettle of your pasture; let us swear
That you are worth your breeding; which I doubt not;
For there is none of you so mean and base,
That hath not noble lustre in your eyes.
I see you stand like greyhounds in the slips,
Straining upon the start.
The game's afoot:
Follow your spirit, and upon this charge
Cry 'God for Harry, England, and Saint George!'

King Henry V
William Shakespeare

Go For Goal!

So, how would you motivate your team? It's half-time and you're one-nil down. Do you:

- **Encourage them:** 'Just keep playing as well as you are and the goals will come ...'

- **Insult and frighten them:** 'You were a bunch of cissy, gutless jerks out there for 45 minutes, running about like headless chickens ...'

- **Try to get them going:** 'Remember how you played against Chelsea and there's £500 each – in cash – if you pull this one off ...'

- **Talk tactics:** 'Go out deeper on the wings and keep the long crosses coming in because their keeper has looked weak in the air twice.'

- **Draw out individuals:** 'Terry, you can do it from midfield. Get the ball out quicker and get behind them faster ...'

- **Suggest violence:** 'Stop that striker before he gets through to the penalty area! Take him down if necessary!'

As a manager, you can say what you like, but you have to achieve results! Footballers, which is what most managers used to be, are good with their feet but not always so good with words. Try these examples!

'I'm not a believer in luck ... but I do believe you need it.'
Alan Ball

'He's very fast and if he gets a yard ahead of himself nobody will catch him.'
Bobby Robson

'I would also think that the action replay showed it to be worse than it actually was.'
Ron Atkinson

'They have missed so many chances they must be wringing their heads in shame.'
Ron Greenwood

'If history is going to repeat itself I should think we can expect the same thing again.'
Terry Venables

'We must have had 99 percent of the game. It was the other three percent that cost us the match.'
Ruud Gullit

Working with a small group, improvise the dressing-room scene at half-time. Each person in the group should have the chance to be the manager and should choose one of the Go for Goal! methods. Afterwards, discuss which approaches worked best.

Next, write an essay comparing at least three of the approaches. Discuss their advantages and disadvantages and say which of them – you can choose more than one – you would use if you were a manager.
OR
Try to describe the qualities of the ideal team manager as you see them.

Guess the Song

Football fans have sung on the terraces and, more recently, in seats, for at least 50 years. Anthropologists (experts who study human behaviour) think that a good chant or song binds a tribe together and gets the warriors excited before battle but it's also a good way to keep warm in November! Travelling to away matches means that new songs travel too and everyone thinks that their version is the original one. However, many of them are libellous and obscene!

The English Euro 96 anthem, 'Three Lions', was a rarity because it was a new song. But why write a new tune when there are so many great old ones? And you can do a lot with the words! Below are some of the cleaner versions – and funny too – of some older songs. You should recognise all the tunes!

Who let the reds out?
Hou Hou Houllier

1

Sign on!
Sign on!
With a pen in your hand,
Coz you'll never get a job!
You'll never get a job ...

2

Don't cry for me,
Aston Villa,
The truth is, we never left you.
All thru' Division 2,
We always followed you,
Now you're the greatest,
Aston Villa.

3

Glory, glory, Leeds United,
Glory, glory, Leeds United,
Glory, glory, Leeds United,
They're the greatest football team in the land.

4

MANAGER'S TIP

One thing you'll notice is how many of these songs can be adapted to suit your own club so you don't need to be very original. Remember also that a good song travels because people hear it, so keep your lyrics simple and clear and don't have too many verses.

You are my Solskjaer,
My Ole Solskjaer,
You make me happy, when skies are grey.
Oh Alan Shearer,
He might be dearer,
but please don't take my Solskjaer away.

I've never felt more like singing the blues,
City win, United lose.
Oh, City,
You got me singing the blues.
Clap clap clap clap

Qué será será!
Whatever will be, will be ...
We're going to Wembley!!
Qué será será ...

And to show that football has a European dimension:

Si t'es fier d'être Parisien
frappe dans tes mains ... clap ... clap ... clap.
Si t'es fier d'être Parisien
frappe dans tes mains ... clap ... clap ... clap.
Si t'es fier d'être Parisien, si t'es fier d'être Parisien, si t'es fier d'être Parisien

Frappe dans tes mains ... clap ... clap ... clap.
Si t'es fier du PSG, frappe dans tes mains ... clap ... clap ... clap.
Si t'es fier du PSG, frappes dans tes mains ... clap ... clap ... clap.
Si t'es fier du PSG, si t'es fier du PSG, si t'es fier du PSG
Frappes dans tes mains ... clap ... clap ... clap.
Paris ... Paris ... Paris

* 'fier' means proud and PSG is the Paris St-Germain football club

Be inspired. Write your own song based on a current hit or an old favourite, or modify one of these to suit your own club and favourite players. Keep it clean or the television companies will blank it out on match days! Make a collection of your local club's current repertoire. Talk to old fans and find out which songs they used to sing.

Just as advances in IT have made it easier to produce fanzines, they have also allowed the clubs to produce smarter and glossier programmes. As well as team information and news, these carry advertising from companies associated with the club. In a typical match programme today, expect to find a comment from the manager, team news, details about the club shops, player profiles and articles about the club's other teams' activities and events.

Go For Goal!

Write a profile of your favourite player for inclusion in a match programme. OR
Design a new strip for the junior team.
Annotate your design to show its interesting new features.

THE MATCH PROGRAMME

FA CARLING PREMIERSHIP

THE FAME GAME
FAMOUS ARSENAL SUPPORTERS SHARE THEIR THOUGHTS AND FEELINGS ABOUT FOLLOWING THE GUNNERS

Arsenal fanatic Dermot O'Leary is one of the country's hottest new TV presenters and can currently be seen on Channel 4's **T4**.

He has also presented *The Barfly Sessions, The Dogs Balearics, The Big Breakfast* and *No Balls Allowed*, all on Channel 4. You can hear Dermot hosting his own radio show on XFM 104.9 every Saturday between 10am and 1pm.

What are your earliest Arsenal memories?
The 1979 FA Cup Final, Brady playing a stormer and going into school the next day feeling very proud. I was one of the only Arsenal fans and (naturally) there were a fair few Man U fans.

What was it that made you become a Gooner?
Mainly the strong Irish contingent when I was growing up. The spine of the team was Irish and so many of the Irish in London supported Arsenal. I always look out for the Celtic result, but Arsenal has always been my team.

Who would you consider your first Highbury hero?
David O'Leary - I used to pretend he was my uncle. In fact I still do!

What qualities did you particularly admire about this player?
Great character, even under pressure, he loved the fans and the club and in my mind helped Adams and Keown become the players they are today.

When we move to a new stadium what aspects of 'The Arsenal Tradition' would you like to be incorporated?
There should be a new Clock End and North Bank and some aspect of the marble halls legacy should also be preserved.

Arsenal to win the Champions League or England to win the World Cup?
I'm Irish so that's easy, but I would like us to win the league before the European Cup.

You have £150M which three players would you bring to Highbury?
Zidane to play alongside Vieira, Dyer from Newcastle, Roy Keane - yeah I know, but I'd rather have him with us than at Man U (maybe Robbie Keane also, but we should focus more on youth rather than big names).

What's the most memorable game you've witnessed involving Arsenal - for the right reasons?
I guess the '89 Liverpool game, sure I wasn't there, but I've never been prouder.

What's the most memorable game you've witnessed involving Arsenal - for the wrong reasons?
The defeat by Man U last season - classic Man U we play them off the pitch for nearly 90 minutes and then Keane scores twice - I was gutted.

List your all time Arsenal XI
Jennings, Dixon, Adams, O'Leary, Sansom, Rocastle, Brady, Vieira, Marwood, Wright, Stapleton.

Has the Arsenal ever impacted on your career and if so how?
Only when people recognise me, if they are a Gooners it's fine, but Spurs fans can be a nightmare.

What are your hopes for the Gunners for the remainder of this season and beyond?
To win the FA cup this year and to see the younger players such as Pennant, Canoville, Barrett and Taylor used in the near future.

Arsenal Football Club

GunnersLine - Live Commentary & Ticket News 0906 474 4444 (Calls cost 60p per minute at all times) 1

MANAGER'S TIP

Look at some examples before you write. Try to capture their style. Once you've chosen a player, an Internet search will turn up lots of details for you to use.

WORDS: ANDY EXLEY

HENRY 14

Thierry HENRY

WORLD CUP WINNER CHAMPIONS THE FA CUP

Thierry Henry loves the FA Cup and his enthusiasm for the World's oldest Cup competition was further bolstered by the magnificent atmosphere at Old Trafford in the semi-final.

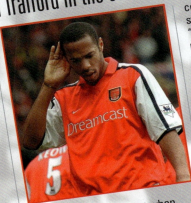

Now Thierry's hoping family and friends from France will join him next Saturday in the Millennium Stadium to sample the special atmosphere for themselves:

"As I said straight after the Tottenham game, I was involved in the French World Cup winning team and I have played in the final of Euro 2000 but I've never heard something like that in my life the noise was so, so, so loud and I would like to play every round against Tottenham in an atmosphere like that, obviously you cannot do that, but what an atmosphere.

"And now I am hoping that a lot of my family will be able to come over for the final, I hope they can, but it is a bit difficult. In this way Wembley would have been better because it's much easier for people to get there, and get hotels and things. Wales is somewhere we don't know much about, but I

the size of the game. But when you are actually in it, when you play this kind of game it is amazing, even Robert and Sylvain have spoken to me about this. "When you play in the Cup in France it is not the same," points out the former Monaco star" but here, when you go onto the pitch it is an extra feeling, a bonus, because the fans make you feel

competition; the former Juventus star agrees:

"Sylvain was playing in the FA Cup more than in the league earlier in the season and give him the chance to play and he will score goals, he is a quality player," says Thierry of the competition's top scorer. "He showed his quality in the competition and that he can be a regular scorer. Of course Robert has also done well too, but you know everyone was talking about the match winning goal of Robert's against Tottenham, but what a cross from Sylvain Wiltord. You have to think first about the cross - then the goal, no-one was in the net, if the ball reached Robert he was always going to score - what a cross!"

Back to the bigger picture, and whilst the Champions League and Premiership Title remained in sight, making smooth progress to the FA Cup final, with no replays

> "...everyone was talking about the match winning goal of Robert's against Tottenham, but what a cross from Sylvain Wiltord."

Arsenal Football Club

will be trying to work-out a way for them all to come because, you know, it is a very big thing.

"People in France," continues Arsenal's leading scorer "they do not realise what the FA Cup means. In England it is normal for you to see an FA Cup game and the stands are completely full, half Arsenal and half Liverpool for example, because you are used to

like this is something that is the most important thing in the world for them."

Important to the fans - most definitely, but a run in the FA Cup can also provide players with a vital opportunity to make a mark at a club and Thierry's French team-mates Robert Pires and in particular Sylvain Wiltord have relished the chance to shine in the

required, was important for the Club:

"I didn't play in the first game at Carlisle, but the lads said it was very hard and though people expected us to win it was a tough start for us. The Chelsea game was always going to be tough as well, a London derby, but we had a great advantage being at home which was crucial for us.

27

FOOTBALL METAPHORS

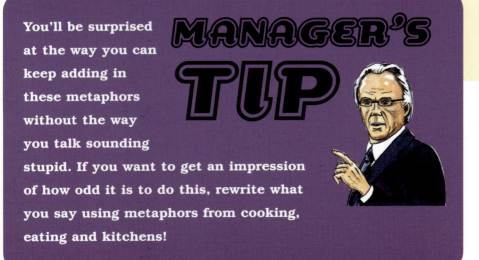

Football has its own rich language. Words and phrases from football have been carried over into other areas of life. If a teacher says to a student 'that's earned you a yellow card', the student knows he or she has been warned. Everyone knows that life is a game of football until the final whistle goes and you can either compete and get stuck in or sit on the bench or the sidelines. In football, and in life, you need to keep the ball in the air, tackle your problems and avoid an early bath! What others can you think of?

The metaphor of football as a battle of life and death rather than a sporting game is used such a lot that we often don't even notice it. But in football you find defence and attack, tactics to win victories, shots on goal, strikers who are weapons in the team's armoury, and the aim is to overwhelm and crush your opponents.

MANAGER'S TIP

You'll be surprised at the way you can keep adding in these metaphors without the way you talk sounding stupid. If you want to get an impression of how odd it is to do this, rewrite what you say using metaphors from cooking, eating and kitchens!

Go For Goal!

Write a manager's team talk using as many 'battle and conflict' metaphors as you can.

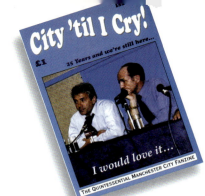

Fanzines are magazines that provide the 'fan on the terrace' with a voice of his or her own, in contrast to the glossy match programme. Almost every club has at least one fanzine now.

Fanzines

Go For Goal!

Produce your own fanzine using cut-and-paste and photocopying or, if you are keen on ICT, using a desktop publishing programme. If you are keener still, develop a fanzine website dedicated to your favourite club.

They are easy to produce using computers and photocopying and are often controversial in what they say. And, now, the dedicated fan can find his or her fanzines online – you don't even have to go to the match!

Looked at in one way, they are an attempt by the fans to have a say about the affairs of the clubs that they invest so much time and money in. However, they have been around for a long time – there was an independent football magazine available in 1882!

Their style was and is influenced by comics, music magazines and underground music. The first modern ones had deliberately provocative names. *Foul* was one of the most famous early fanzines and, after it collapsed, *Sick as a Parrot* took over. This was published every two months and cost 20p a copy and can claim to be one of the first modern football fanzines.

MANAGER'S TIP

Don't be over ambitious. Keep it simple and straight-forward. If you can, get hold of some fanzines to give you some ideas of what to include.

MORE IMPORTANT THINGS THAN FOOTBALL

In 1914, Britain was at war with Germany but the battle was deadlocked with the two sides occupying trenches and the deadly no man's land in between. Hundreds of thousands of young men had already died in hand-to-hand fighting that gained only hundreds of yards of territory. And tactical errors by the generals and the introduction of mustard gas and the machine gun meant that this was a world of horrors for the common soldier.

At Christmas 1914, and again in 1915, something happened across the Front. Nobody knows exactly what but there was some kind of unofficial truce. Here are some eye-witness accounts:

The mist was slow to clear and suddenly my orderly threw himself into my dug-out to say that both German and Scottish soldiers had come out of their trenches and were fraternising and exchanging cigarettes, schnapps and chocolate. Later a Scottish soldier appeared with a football which seemed to come from nowhere and a few minutes later a real football match got underway. The Scots marked their goal mouth with their strange caps and we did the same. It was far from easy to play on the frozen ground, but we continued, keeping rigorously to the rules, despite the fact that it only lasted an hour and that we had no referee. Us Germans really roared when a gust of wind revealed that the Scots wore nothing under their kilts. The game finished with a score of three goals to two in favour of Fritz against Tommy.

Leutnant Johannes Niemann, 133rd Saxon Regiment, German army

We were only 100 yards or so apart when Christmas morning came. A German began singing 'All Through The Night', then more voices joined in and the British troops responded with 'Good King Wenceslas '... the next morning, all the soldiers were shouting to one another, 'Hello Tommy, Hello Fritz' ... The Germans started it, coming out of their trenches and walking over to us. Nobody decided for us – we just climbed over our parapet and went over to them, we thought nobody would shoot at us if we all mingled together ... There wouldn't have been a war if it had been left to the public. We didn't want to fight but we thought we were defending England.

Bertie Felstead, then a 21-year-old Welsh Fusilier, died 2001, aged 106.

Baldrick: And then, shortly after, we all met up, didn't we? Just before Christmas, 1914.

George: Yes, that's right. I'd just arrived and we had that wonderful Christmas truce. Do you remember, sir? We could hear 'Silent Night' drifting across the still, clear air of no man's land. And then they came, the Germans, emerging out of the freezing night mist, calling to us, and we clambered up over the top and went to meet them.

Blackadder: Both sides advanced more during one Christmas piss-up than they managed in the next two-and-a-half years of war.

Baldrick: Do you remember the football match?

Blackadder: Remember it? How could I forget it? I was never offside! I could not believe that decision!

Blackadder Goes Forth: BBC TV: script by Ben Elton and Richard Curtis

---

Go For Goal!

Ask your history teacher for more details about the Christmas truces in the 1914–18 war. See what else you can find out about them using your school library or an Internet search engine. Make up your own mind about what is true and what may just be exaggerations and stories, and write a report of your findings.

MANAGER'S TIP

Think about who your report could be for. A school website, a magazine, a local paper? Knowing who your audience is will help you to write. If you're using the Internet, use an international search engine like Google.com and use First World War, 'Christmas truce', football as your key words. (Putting Christmas truce in quotation marks stops you receiving everything there is on Santa Claus!)

Computer Football

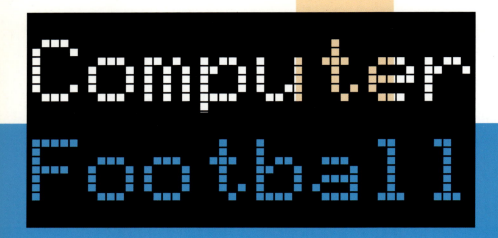

One way that millions of people play football is on games consoles. Nowadays you can watch and play football virtually and it can make you just as excited and angry. The games are so sophisticated that you can play football in a range of countries and leagues, identify individual players and have match commentaries as you go along!

Writing reviews used to be a careful activity where you gave a balanced view but, for computer games, anything goes.

Go For Goal!

Do some research to find out what soccer games are currently available and what your friends like about them, and then write your own review for a teenage magazine.

Premier World Soccer

Year: 1994   Publisher: Sportsvision

When Premier World Soccer first arrived … it literally offered a new angle on the football genre. The isometric camera position, cool 'n' chunky-looking players plus a generous helping of spectacular moves like overhead kicks and searing 30-yard shots the like of which had never previously been seen in a console game. Premier World Soccer is far from perfect, but you have to go back and play some of the older versions to see how truly bad it was. Even now, many of the latest version's flaws can be traced back to the … original. When it first came out, the brash arcade approach coupled with excellent presentation was enough to win over many a player, not to mention establish one of the most lucrative and successful games franchises ever in the process. After seven years and eight updates you'd expect them to have got things right.

International League Football

Year: 2000   Publisher: Softball Inc.

It's been a long time coming, but finally there's a game on a next generation console to rival real soccer for sheer playability combined with the 3-D graphics demanded by today's gamers. ISS Pro Evolution is the latest in a long line of ISS games, all of which have had some great ideas and features. Here, for the first time, it all comes together to create the most realistic, tactical and flexible football game ever produced. While the FIFA game is driven by people more interested in what song plays over the intro sequence than how the game plays, ISS lets the football do the talking, and it's time you started listening!

Trust me, you need this game, not only is it the best football game on PS1 it is also the best on PS2. As a games player for over 15 years this is the only game I can play time after time and not get slightly bored with it. So no bad points? Sadly yes (nothing is perfect). Even though Konami have the licence from FIFA to use real names, they still make mistakes. The names of some of the South American players are wrong – Rivaldo is Rivadoh – and the commentary is awful. What's worse is that the gameplay is noticeably slower than in the last version. However, none of this detracts from the most playable game available today. If it were a footballer it would be Pele, as opposed to FIFA – which would be Stan Collymore.

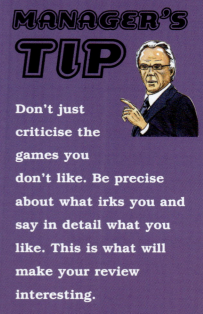

MANAGER'S TIP

Don't just criticise the games you don't like. Be precise about what irks you and say in detail what you like. This is what will make your review interesting.

Arguing about FOOTBALL

It's possible that football is the most discussed and argued-over subject in the British Isles. At work, in bars and cafes and on Saturdays in the season, everyone talks about football. Football is social glue. If you meet someone new, how long does it take to ask them what team they support? And it's funny, but you'll normally say something good about that team even when they're your team's worst enemy – especially if you like the person! Do you know what you're doing? You're bonding! Becoming friends because you have a common interest.

With friends, arguments about football can be exciting, ferocious and passionate. So what do you think about foreign players in the Premier League? The thing is that whatever age or sex you are, you can't help but have an opinion! This is the argument from Soccer Centre, an Internet site for soccer enthusiasts.

Soccer Centre takes time to argue over the increasing demand for foreign imports to be limited to six per club. We couldn't decide which side to support and it nearly caused a fist fight in the office so Editor Ed and Editor Luke put their own sides of the story.

THE CASE FOR FOREIGN IMPORTS

Ten years ago if anybody tried to argue that the English premiership (or as it was then the First Division) was the most exciting in the world or even in Europe, they would have been laughed off the football pitch. Nowadays, it is far more debatable, our top division is highly regarded and it produces some of the best (if not the best) teams in the world. There has been a massive increase in the standards of football in the English premiership in recent years as a consequence of an influx of foreign imports. Chelsea and Arsenal in particular have boasted some of the best foreigners in the world. The skills of players like Zola, Bergkamp, Desailly, Petit and Viera, to name just a few, have entertained English fans no end.

THE CASE AGAINST FOREIGN IMPORTS

Fact. The best team in the country/Europe is Manchester United. Fact. Man United's first eleven includes Gary Neville, David Beckham, Paul Scholes, Andy Cole and Ryan Giggs who are all British. Manchester United has proven that a great team includes Englishmen. Look at Chelsea when Dennis Wise isn't playing and the difference that young Jody Morris made against Barcelona.

In the long term, investment in young English players can provide greater success then a reliance on foreigners whose loyalty to the premiership may not be as strong. English football may benefit at the International level because of what the English players learn from their foreign colleagues but an influx of foreigners also prevents more potential England internationals from demonstrating what they can do at the highest club level.

However, the most devastating consequence of the flood of foreigners is how it is crippling the smaller clubs because the big clubs no longer need to buy players from the smaller clubs. Foreigners are cheaper. Overall, the consequences of the foreign invasion clearly outweigh the advantages. A limit on the number of foreigners is the only solution.

Go For Goal!

Whose side are you on? Talk about the issues in a small group and then write your own view as a persuasive argument. It could be as a letter to a sports magazine or an e-mail to a football website.
Never arrange to meet anyone you write to or e-mail on a website on your own.

MANAGER'S TIP

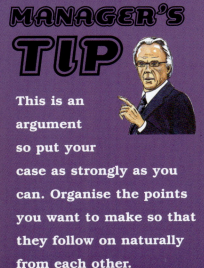

This is an argument so put your case as strongly as you can. Organise the points you want to make so that they follow on naturally from each other.

35

Football Issues

There's a debate at the moment about whether the ordinary fans get a fair deal from their clubs. Replica kits are expensive, season ticket prices are rocketing and the conditions at many grounds (refreshments, toilets, car-parking, queues) put many people off, especially when they see businessmen in the hospitality boxes enjoying the best views of the game.

What would football be like … if the fans started to leave? Here is one discussion of the issues.

How popular would football be if it was played in half-empty stadiums? Would the clubs introduce canned cheering and pre-recorded chants? And what would television do? Fake the atmosphere? Create virtual supporters and get live extras to sit in the front-row seats? Would the players be as committed and passionate as they are now? Or would it all become a money-fuelled pantomime?

Why do we ask these questions? Because there is a real danger that the sport of football is forgetting who makes it so special. In the mad rush to achieve success and thus earn more television money, the most successful clubs seem to be forgetting who their real supporters are. There is much

talk of fans as customers – you can buy all manner of season tickets, replica kits and merchandise – but in reality many clubs treat their loyal fans more like cash machines.

However big the cheques for television rights, the fans are, and always will be, the most important source of income for a club. They will be there when the team is less successful. They will be there if the broadcasters start to spend their money elsewhere.

Or will they? Many fans now feel short-changed and overlooked. People are asking questions. Where are the rights that go with being a customer? Why do fans still have to put up with substandard facilities, endless queuing and being spoken down to whenever they disagree with the club? Why should following a club cost so much money?

And what of the future? With the bigger clubs getting all the hype, what of the next

generation of supporters for the supposedly 'less glamorous' outfits? Will younger fans really go to see their local heroes play when they can watch superstars on the telly or interact with their computer games instead?

From top to bottom, football needs to look at what attracts people to the game and how the sport's supporters could be better treated. If the fans start leaving football one thing is for sure – television will be right behind them.

MANAGER'S TIP

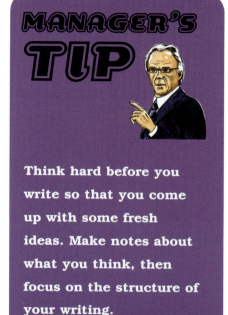

Think hard before you write so that you come up with some fresh ideas. Make notes about what you think, then focus on the structure of your writing.

Go For Goal!

What's your view of the future of football? Will the game go on getting bigger and bigger or will the bubble burst? Do you think it is right that clubs should change their strip every season simply to make the fans buy highly priced shirts? Do you think that the fans get a fair deal?

Write an essay giving your opinions on how the game will develop. OR Describe a big football game in 2020, showing what changes will have taken place by then.

OOTBALL CLUB PLC

rson Ticket

NED

HOOLIGANS

Bad and antisocial behaviour at football matches has been an issue for football for many years. Since a major problem emerged in the 1970s with English fans travelling overseas, the police have worked hard to identify trouble-makers. Banning individuals from grounds, banning alcohol on trains, closing pubs, using closed circuit television in stadiums and monitoring the approaches to grounds have been effective in making football a safer game for the average spectator. Some people think that this is unfair and that the police confuse enthusiasm with lawbreaking. Read this poem and the two extracts that follow and think about how you feel about the issue.

Fan

I'm a football fan but I must admit
That I sometimes act like a brainless git
Like a lager lout or a loud half-wit
Or a totally typical drunken Brit.

But I'm genuine, not a counterfeit.
And I might just lark about a bit
And shove and shout and refuse to sit
But football fans are proud of it.

We wear the legitimate scarf and kit.
It's a bright outfit, so it's no secret.
We're football fans for definite.
We're a rowdy crowd but we're proud of it.

It's a game of guile and grace and grit,
A spirited sport for the physically fit.
With my season ticket in my mitt,
I'm a football fan and I'm proud of it.

With literally little that's not been writ,
I can only add that I'll never quit.
I'm a football fan, not a hypocrite,
A football fan and I'm proud of it.

Nick Toczek

The use of video cameras, the decrease in crowds and the huge numbers and better organisation of the police now make it impossible to have a punch-up and remain anonymous, which has always been so important to the hooligan. The early outbreaks of violence were totally connected with the match itself – a goal being scored or a penalty award – and the threat of violence existed only inside the ground or in its immediate vicinity. Now, though, it seems that violence can erupt anywhere, and people are often attacked up to three hours before or after a match. It has become organised gang violence, with tactics and weapons entering the picture, and the fast attack mentality prevails: get in fast, do the damage and get out again. The grounds have become like caged fortresses, and although the police tactics are generally good, all they seem to have achieved is to transfer the violence elsewhere.

When I was a young man, getting punched in the mouth at football seemed just a part of growing up. There were definitely more fights on the terraces in the 1970s than there are now, but as the match punch-ups have declined, so the violence has moved on and become more serious. There is increasing use of knives in football violence. There were isolated stabbings at matches when I was in my teens, but the carrying of a knife was a rarity; it was considered almost unmanly. Now, it seems that every confrontation ends in a stabbing, and that is pretty frightening.

Everyone has their own theories, but the fact is that football is simply a mirror reflection of society – at least, that's certainly true of this country. The level of violence in

our society, whatever its cause, has been reflected at football matches for the last 20 years. Football has been seen as an ideal vehicle by groups of young adolescents wanting to express themselves, and they consider their behaviour perfectly normal and acceptable. Football fans, like every other group of people, are only conforming to the practices of their own group. It is similar to upper-class public schoolboys playing polo, or young debutantes attending coming-out balls. Politicians throw up their hands in horror at hooliganism, yet consider the way they themselves behave in the House of Commons: so-called civilised people verbally abusing, chanting at, obstructing, interrupting and even occasionally physically

assaulting each other. It sounds very much like a football crowd to me. And at least football crowds applaud the opposition sometimes!

I look back on my time on the terraces as an apprenticeship, part of the learning process, but just as children tend to grow out of asthma, so I grew out of my youthful behaviour. Some people don't however, and the use of weapons in football violence now by men in their late twenties and early thirties (some of them parents themselves) is a frightening fact of life. When the police catch these knife-wielding thugs, young or old, I believe they should be locked up for a long time.

Steaming In Colin Ward

Go For Goal!

Answer these questions to help you focus on the issue.

- How does Colin Ward think that hooliganism has changed? Look for at least three ways.

- What does he mean when he says that hooliganism is simply a reflection of changes in our society?

- How does his view of today's hooligans differ from the picture given by the poem?

- How does Dougie Brimson suggest that hooligans are not simply violent thugs?

- Explain how Dougie Brimson compares hooligans to drunk drivers.

Next, write a story about a football hooligan where what starts as 'a bit of fun' leads to serious consequences. OR Write a short essay about what measures you would encourage to stamp out bad behaviour among football fans. Think about how you might stop bad behaviour before it starts.

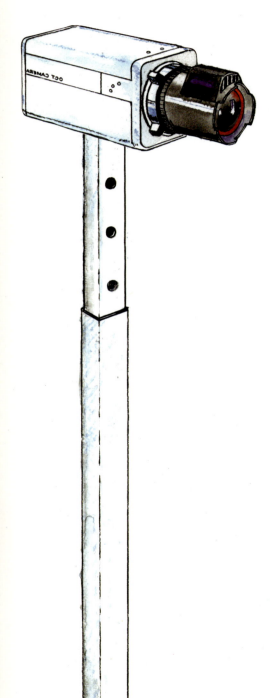

There is also a certain code of honour among the firms (gangs of hooligans), one which draws specific boundaries marking what is and is not acceptable behaviour. For example, if you and your lads received a battering at the hands of a rival mob, you do not go to the police and complain about it, you simply exact revenge next time around. That's the way it works. But for many of the individuals involved, the fact that these boundaries are in place seems to reinforce the belief that hooliganism is nothing more than a game. Violence for the sake of it might not be attractive, but kicking things off with another group of hooligans who will also adhere to the rules is not looked down upon in quite the same way, either by those who inflict it or those who suffer as a result. Furthermore, many of those involved simply do not consider what they do to be wrong in any legal sense, because to a large extent among football fans hooliganism has never really been criminalised.

A comparison can be made with drink-driving. Most of us have either done did at one time or know someone who has, and we all know that it's against the law. Yet if we see someone leaving the pub who is clearly over the limit, do we shop them? No, we don't, because drink-driving still isn't regarded as a 'proper' crime and if the bloke gets caught, we think of him as being unlucky. Yet if he runs someone over, we quite rightly condemn him out of hand because then, he really has broken a law that everyone would regard as 'proper'. Hooliganism is exactly the same. For many, that isn't a 'proper' crime either. If we know who the people involve are, do we shop them? Almost certainly not, we are more likely just to think of them as lads. Yet in reality, football hooliganism is nothing more than violent, premeditated crime but because of this apathy towards it from many football fans, the people involved carry on their activities pretty much unmolested and are able to justify their behaviour to themselves because no one else seems to care. For some people, it is actually the getting away with it that is the main attraction. Only when they end up in court, and the anonymity they have enjoyed is removed, does the full realisation – and consequences – of what they have been doing, as well as risking, hit home. The sad reality, however, is that very few of the people involved in hooliganism will ever end up in court. They will simply carry on until they drift out of direct involvement after a few years because of age or boredom.

Barmy Army Dougie Brimson

MANAGER'S TIP

Try to reflect the complexity of the issue in your writing. Every hooligan was once a sweet little baby! Think about where society and its attitudes might be more supportive.

RACISM

One of the worst features of modern football is racism. Clubs strive to stop it, making it clear that anyone making racist comments will be thrown out of the ground. Television commentaries might conceal it from the viewer but the unfortunate truth is that it still goes on. This is writer Nick Hornby's description of one encounter with the problem.

… we could see quite clearly, as the teams warmed up before the kick-off, that banana after banana was being hurled from the away supporters' enclosure. The bananas were designed to announce, for the benefit of those unversed in codified terrace abuse, that there was a monkey on the pitch; and as the Liverpool fans have never bothered to bring bananas to previous Arsenal matches, even though we have always had at least one black player in the side since the turn of the decade, one can only assume that John Barnes was the monkey to whom they were referring.

Those who have seen John Barnes, this beautiful, elegant man, play football, or give an interview, or even simply walk out on to a pitch, and have also stood next to the grunting, overweight orang-utans who do things like throw bananas and make a monkey noises, will

appreciate the irony of all this … It was a revolting, nauseating sight.

Arsenal, by and large, have no problems with this kind of filth any more, although they have problems of other kinds, particularly anti-Semitism. There are black fans on the terraces and in the seats and our

best players … are black and enormously popular. That said, you can still, even now, occasionally hear of idiots who jeer the black players on opposing teams. (One night I turned round angrily to confront an Arsenal fan making monkey noises at Manchester United's Paul Ince and found that I was abusing a blind man. A blind racist!)

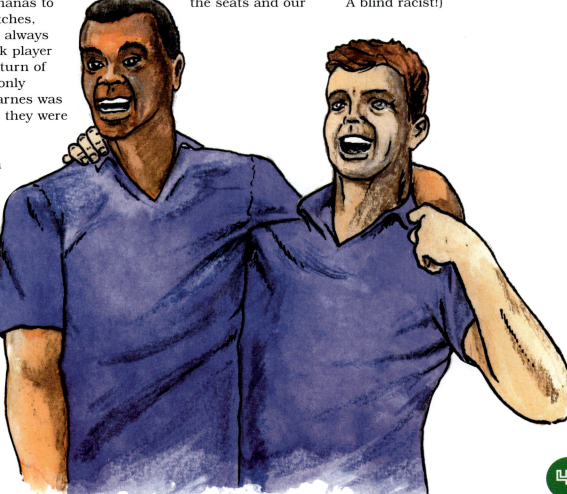

... It seems lame to say that I loathe the baiting of black players that takes place as a matter of routine inside some football grounds, and if I had any guts I would have either (a) confronted some of the worst perpetrators or (b) stopped going to games. Before remonstrating with the blind racist I was making some frantic calculations – how hard is he? How hard are his mates? How hard are my mates? – until I heard something, a certain whininess in his voice, maybe, that led me to conclude I wasn't about to get a pasting, and I acted accordingly but this is rare. More usually I take the view that these people, like those who smoke on tube trains, know what they're doing, and their abuse is intended to intimidate anyone, black or white, who feels like doing something about it.

Fever Pitch Nick Hornby

JOHN BARNES

How would you feel if you heard racist or homophobic comments directed at you from your own club's fans? Imagine that you are a black footballer making your debut for a new club. Describe what happens and how you feel about it. What do your team mates say? Is it possible to stop it?

MANAGER'S TIP

Maybe you have experienced racist comments for yourself and know how hurtful and unpleasant they can be or, perhaps, you've found yourself making them in the past.

Draw on your own experiences to make the feelings in your writing as genuine as possible. You could write a poem to do this.

Football FICTION

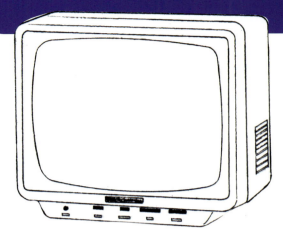

From *Roy of the Rovers* to *Dream Team*, football fans have always wanted to read strip cartoons and stories about the game or watch television programmes and films. Footballers are celebrities now and their lives outside football are often seen as being as interesting as what they do on the pitch.

Here's a profile of one imaginary player:

Jason Cragg is only 23 and has been in the first team at Welby United since his £14 million transfer from Italian club Lazio – but he hasn't settled in too well. His form has only been so-so and his film star wife Donatella isn't happy living in London. He has been playing in a rock band with his friend Ali and some newspaper reporters think that he is not properly committed to the club. He likes to go clubbing and has been photographed coming out of Abigail's at 4.00am with Kanga Roux, the Australian popstar.

Write another two profiles. The first is of the tough Welby United Manager who is worried that his job could be on the line if Jason doesn't succeed and the second the old team captain and Welby stalwart who thinks that these young celebrity footballers need taking down a peg or two.

Next, either draw a cartoon strip or write a scene for a television script showing how a conflict develops between the three characters and how it is finally resolved. You can bring in additional characters as well, of course.

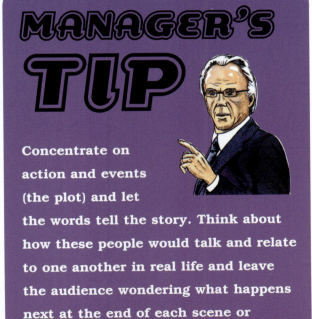

MANAGER'S TIP

Concentrate on action and events (the plot) and let the words tell the story. Think about how these people would talk and relate to one another in real life and leave the audience wondering what happens next at the end of each scene or picture sequence.

Will Knight's dilemma

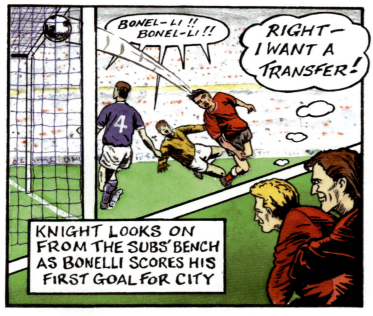

GIRLS V BOYS

Women's and girls' football is now well organised even if on a much smaller scale than the men's game. Many of the top clubs have women's and girls' teams, for example, and there are national league and cup competitions. But is thinking that girls have just got to 'join the party' missing the point? Read this article by Robin Marantz Henig, an American writer. It is about the game in the USA, there may be lessons here for us all.

When the coaches running our soccer program first suggested forming an all-girls division, the girls thought it was a terrible idea. Our daughter Samantha, who is 10, had been playing on the co-ed league for three years, and that's where she wanted to stay. I was suspicious of the change as well. Was this new division an admission that girls just can't cut it when they try to play with the Big Boys? Would the best players in an all-girls league inevitably feel that, no matter how good they are, they are somehow and forever second-string?

There was no doubt that, in mixed-sex soccer, the girls and the boys played two different games. The females co-operated; the males aggressed. The girls played their positions, waiting for the ball to come into their territory before passing it to a team mate. The boys, meanwhile, catapulted toward the ball in a mass of legs and torsos, no matter where it was, and fought even their own team mates for the right to kick it as hard and as far as they could.

The girls, in short, played by the rules and acted as members of a team, while the boys charged ahead ferociously. It seemed a metaphor for the way the male of the species solves most problems, physical or intellectual: by using speed and strength rather than strategy or intuition. On reflection, then, I had to concede that the all-girls league was worth a try. Maybe it was time, after all, to give the girls their own playing field.

Sam objected to playing in the new division; she thought it was sexist to separate the girls from the boys. But the first game showed my husband and me how right we had been to insist that she try it, sexist or not. With no boys to steal their thunder, the girls were suddenly terrific. The soccer they played was fast and aggressive, even better than the boys' because they still remembered to play their positions and pass. It was a revelation.

When Sam's team finished the season undefeated (five wins, four ties), they actually challenged an all-boys team to an exhibition game. (They weren't total fools, though; the team they chose to play had an average age about a year younger than theirs.) 'How will those boys feel if they end up getting beaten by girls?' Jane's (a friend's) husband asked her before the game. Her answer: 'Get used to it.'

Go For Goal!

What do you make of this article? Do you think girls should have separate football leagues? Do you agree with Robin that they end up playing a different game? Write a letter to Robin giving your views.

45

And beaten they were. Our girls prevailed, with a score of one to nothing. Okay, maybe their extra height turned out to be an unfair advantage, but I like to think what really swung the game was the extra confidence that had been blossoming all season long. As I watched that glorious soccer season unfold, I found myself making the mental leap from the soccer field to the classroom. If girls did so well athletically once they switched from co-ed soccer, would the same thing happen academically if they switched from co-ed schools? Are boys as likely to dominate and reshape what goes on in an academic discussion as they are to distort what goes on in a soccer play?

Sam and her buddies at age 10 are brave, confident feminists. They see sex stereotyping everywhere, and their favourite phrase is, 'That's not fair.' But many experts tell us that, as adolescence approaches, these powerful, egalitarian young women will turn coy and insecure, downplaying their strength and power to get along in a male-dominated society.

In my heart, I worry that the experts might be right. I believe I've seen evidence of their theory during this triumphant soccer season. When the girls were on their own, I saw their transformation with my own eyes – a transformation that might just as easily occur in a single-sex classroom. The girls were more confident, more competent, more free than they had ever been when they were playing in the shadows of the boys.

MANAGER'S TIP

Draw two columns with the headings pros and cons. Make a list of points under each heading. When you turn these lists into a letter, don't forget to include observations from your own experience.

More information

- For more soccer anagrams visit www.extraordinaryworld.com

- For poems visit www.footballpoets.org which is always delighted to receive football poems on-line (poems@footballpoets.org) and is very user-friendly. The poets are always keen to work with schools. Contact the Football Poets, 4 The Retreat, Butterow, Stroud, Glos GL5 2LS or go through the website.

- Or, visit www.footballpoets.com for more poets.

- www.bigfanof.com and www.soccer-centre.org.uk are excellent soccer websites.

- For more about soccer games and simulations, try www.amazon.com

Acknowledgements

1. *Vinnie: The Autobiography* Vinnie Jones, Hodder Headline (1998) ISBN 07472 5914 3 p184.

2. 'The Ghost of Stanley Matthews' and 'What's so wrong about wanting to marry a Big soccer star' by Crispin Thomas © 2000 can be found on the football poets website (poems@footballpoets.org) as above.

3. 'Referee' and 'Stadium' by Ian McMillan © and be found on www.ian-mcmillan.co.uk

4. Photo © Simon Thackeray

5. 'Falling From Grace In The Eyes Of A Child' by Tony Lewis-Jones © 2000 can be found on the football poets website.

6. Carly Spencer, Chandelle Joynes and Louise Gardner are all pupils at Brockworth School and their poems can be found on the football poets website.

7. Thanks to the following fanzines:
Leyton Orienteer, (Leyton Orient), *City 'til I Cry!* (Manchester City), *Macc,* (Macclesfield Town), *Seagulls,* (Brighton & Hove Albion).

8. The computer game reviews come from www.amazon.com

9. The arguments about foreign imports are © Soccer Centre Media 2000 and the soccer-centre website, www.soccer-centre.org.uk

10. 'Fan' by Nick Toczek © 2000 can be found on the football poets website.

11. *Steaming In* by Colin Ward is published by Simon and Schuster UK Ltd, ISBN 0671853651 p181 Copyright © Colin Ward, 1994

12. *Barmy Army* by Dougie Brimson, Hodder Headline (2000) ISBN 07472 6305 1 p71.

13. *Fever Pitch* by Nick Hornby, Gollancz 1992, Penguin 2000. ISBN 0 140 29344 2 Pages 181–182.

14. Robin Marantz Henig can be contacted at www.nasw.org/users/robinhenig/